IMAGES OF ENGLAND

AROUND
SHELDON

IMAGES OF ENGLAND

AROUND SHELDON

MARGARET D. GREEN

TEMPUS

Frontispiece: Guide post at Elmdon airport in 1952.

First published 2004

Tempus Publishing Limited
The Mill, Brimscombe Port,
Stroud, Gloucestershire, GL5 2QG
www.tempus-publishing.com

British Library Cataloguing in Publication Data.
A catalogue record for this book is available from the British Library.

ISBN 0 7524 3363 6

Typesetting and origination by Tempus Publishing Limited.
Printed in Great Britain.

Contents

Going home by bus in the 1950s.

Acknowledgements

All the photographs, except those listed below, are from collections held at Birmingham Central Library. I would particularly like to thank the ladies of Sheldon Women's Institute for their splendid photographic survey of Sheldon in 1967, which was subsequently donated to the library service. Unfortunately I have been unable to identify or trace other donors of photographs or copies which I have included in the book. Whoever you are, thank you.

The following have kindly given permission for their photographs to be used (page locations are given with position, top or bottom, marked as a or b): Sheldon Community Library (15a, 23b, 26a, 29a, 39a, 48b, 68b, 69, 73a, 80a); Colin Giles (17a, 29b, 35a, 92a); Margaret Courbet (82b, 83a, 84a); Anthony Spettigue (33b, 43b); Steve Nelson at Sheldon Country Park (23a); William Gumbley (73a); Colin Simpson (37b); Lithograve Ltd (108b, 110b, 111a); Christine Hampson (108a, 109b); the Midlands Co-operative Society Ltd (74a).

My thanks also to Adrian Neild at Sheldon Community Library, Paul Taylor and Martin Hampson at Birmingham Central Library and to my sister, Susan Abson, for her help with the typing.

Introduction

Sheldon is the nearest Birmingham suburb to the airport, National Exhibition Centre, Birmingham International railway station and the M42 for access to the national motorways. From the boundary at Elmdon, the city centre is only six miles along the A45 Coventry Road. Few travellers on this road will know that only half a mile from the busy shops and office blocks at the Wheatsheaf lies Sheldon's old village, still in semi-rural surroundings. Old cottages are scattered around the medieval church of St Giles, itself backing onto the sprawling acres of Sheldon Country Park. The old parish boundary was roughly defined by water in the north and east, by the River Cole at Tile Cross, Kingshurst Brook at Marston Green and Hatchford Brook across the Elmdon Turnpike, which became the A45. Lyndon End, covering the area between Manor House Lane, Barrows Lane and the Coventry Road was a detached part of the distant parish of Bickenhill until 1874, when it became part of Solihull for the next sixty years.

Sheldon's earliest known settlers were the Anglo-Saxons at Mackadown in the north, where natural springs and light soils made primitive farming easy. Their leader was Macca, who gave his name to the area, Machitone or Macca's farm, and it was under this name that the district was recorded in the Domesday survey in 1086.

The later name of Sheldon derived from the Scheldon family who were lords of the manor from 1220. Further settlement occurred south of the low-lying, damp and peaty Radley Moor, around the area where the church now stands. Before the end of the fourteenth century Sheldon was divided into two manors, East Hall and West Hall. East Hall manor house still exists as Sheldon Hall in Tile Cross, but West Hall at Kent's Moat was a ruin by 1700. At this time almost every family had land for subsistence farming but by 1840 however, 75 per cent of the land was owned by one man, Earl Digby, Lord of the Sheldon Manors. Sheldon remained a farming district until the 1930s and only then did the population exceed 500.

Sheldon was formally incorporated into Birmingham in 1931, to be developed as a residential area, providing homes for people from the overcrowded and squalid central districts of the city. The urbanization of Sheldon had already begun in the 1920s with private housing spreading from the Coventry Road into the Sheaf Lane area. In the 1930s new private estates were built at Cockshutt Hill, Lyndon Green and Cranes Park. Large municipal estates were planned for the north, at Sheldon Heath and Tile Cross, where new roads and drainage systems were already underway when the Second World War began. The war had little direct impact on Sheldon itself and its residents were more at risk working in the factories at Small Heath and Tysley. The only local site of industrial importance was the Metro-Cammell shadow factory at Marston Green, making Stirling bombers. Italian and German prisoners of war worked on local farms or building roads, the latter sometimes bombed by German pilots thinking they were airport runways. Silvermere Road school and some nearby houses suffered bomb damage during the Blitz of 1941 and cattle were killed when a bomb fell on Lower Barn Farm.

After 1945 Sheldon developed rapidly as a residential district. Hundreds of temporary prefabricated dwellings were erected, many still inhabited in the early 1970s while permanent houses were at last built around them. Housing had to be a priority but as a result residents complained about the lack of shops, schools and buses and the poor telephone system and postal service. There were few meeting places for social events, leaving only the pubs for entertainment, or a difficult journey into the city centre. Pre-war settlers had made similar complaints but they had liked the rural feel of the district and enjoyed the simpler life. Home baking was routine but essential groceries could be bought from the few shops at Lyndon End, and local farmers delivered milk and eggs by pony and trap. For those who lived near the village, there were social evenings at the Institute, playing cards or dominoes, and the occasional Saturday dance. For children there was wasteland everywhere for football and cricket and on Bank Holidays and summer Sundays whole families made the long walk to Chelmsley Wood.

Sheldon today is a sprawling residential suburb without a centre. Public services such as the police and the fire stations, public library and neighbourhood office are dispersed throughout. Small manufacturing and trading companies are confined to the Mackadown Lane and Granby Avenue estates. Along the Coventry Road more offices and hotels seem set to replace shops and houses up to Lyndon End. The Metro transport system is to be developed between the airport and the city centre in the next decade, to improve access for residents and visitors. In the age of the car and computer, the lack of local entertainment matters less. Old Sheldon has become a convenient place to live, ideal for commuting throughout the region and the country.

Sheldon has few claims to fame. Its only historically famous resident was Thomas Bray, the Rector of Sheldon, who was nevertheless absent for long periods of time, promoting charity schools, free libraries, missionary work and the education of slaves. In the late 1950s Sheldon was the subject of a research project by local amateurs, the first of its kind in the city. The adult education classes were lead by Victor Skipp, then teaching at Sheldon Heath School, whose pamphlet *Discovering Sheldon* was based on the research. It would have been difficult to write this introduction without it. Also of great use to me have been the compilations of Sheldon references made by Colin Giles from newspapers, directories and parish records.

I hope this selection of photographs successfully shows the changes to Sheldon since the late nineteenth century and that readers find here something of interest and surprise.

Margaret D. Green
August 2004

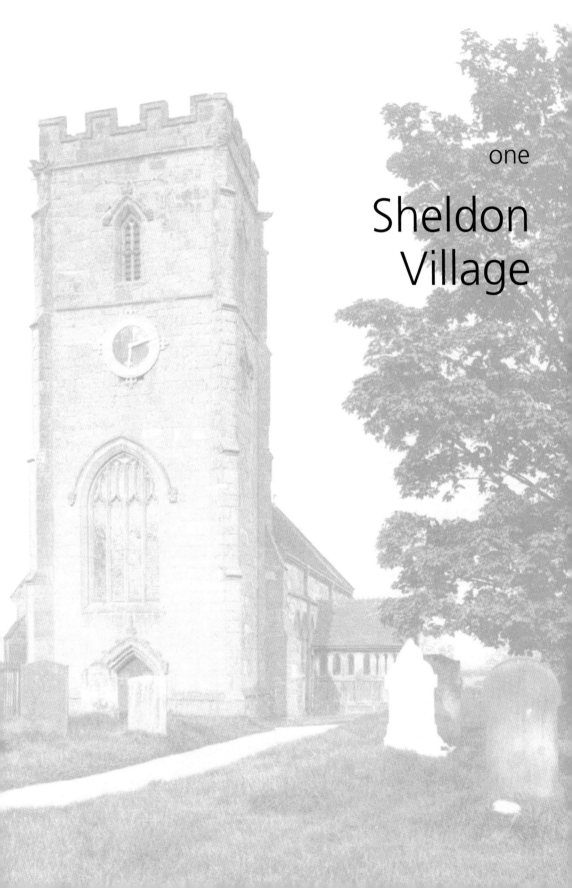

one

Sheldon
Village

SHELDON CHURCH

Above: Church interior, *c.* 1920. The nave is the oldest surviving part of the building, retaining its original wooden roof trusses. The chancel at the end, and the north aisle on the left, were wholly rebuilt in 1867 but this has not affected the medieval feel of the building.

Opposite above: St Giles' church, 1891. There was a church on this site by 1260, but the present building of red sandstone dates from 1330. The tower was added in 1461 and the attractive timber framed porch in the early 1500s.

Opposite below: A side view of the church around 1930, a view hidden today by a thick hedge. The master mason responsible for the tower was Henry Ulm, who also built the towers and steeples of the parish churches of Yardley and Kings Norton.

William Adams, bellringer, caretaker, doorkeeper and sexton, in his beadle uniform, 1887. One of a sexton's duties was to arrange the digging of graves. A church beadle was responsible for summoning parishioners to vestry meetings to discuss parish business. A plaque inside the church commemorates Mr Adams forty-eight years' service to the parish, from 1858 to 1906.

Left: Sunday school pupils, 1911.

Below: The church choir, *c.* 1950.

The lychgate, 1925. This was erected in 1899 and bears a later carved inscription commemorating the sixty-one years served as rector by John Burleton Jones-Bateman. The pair of cottages just visible through the gate were originally the Ring o' Bells inn, also known as the Lamb. They survived until the 1960s.

Pupils and teachers of Sheldon church school, 1914. The first proper school was opened in 1704 and was one of the 1500 charity schools founded by the Society for the Propagation of Christian Knowledge. A leading member of this movement was Thomas Bray, vicar of Sheldon from 1690 to 1729.

The 1852 school and modern church hall viewed from the tower, 1967. The school of 1704 was demolished in 1858. The church school closed in 1937 when new council schools at Stanville Road and Cockshutt Hill were opened.

An old house on the corner of Church Road and Horrell Road, 1967. Still standing, this was the schoolmaster's residence in the late nineteenth century.

The eighteenth-century cottages by the lychgate, 1967.

The church and Institute, *c.* 1925. The Institute was built at the expense of Mrs Annie Grenville in memory of her late husband, who had a sports outfitters business in Birmingham. It opened in 1923 as a workingmen's institute but was used by the whole community for recreational activities. It is now a Royal Air Force meeting hall.

Old cottages next to the Institute in Ragley Drive, 1967. In 1841 they were occupied by Edward Newell, the schoolmaster and parish clerk, and John Price, a farm worker.

Church Road, near the church, 1919. In the distance are the Ring o' Bells cottages. On the left, the nearest house is still known locally as the smithy. A smithying business began here about 1845 but these houses date from about 1860.

Victorian bier cart, 1985. It was made by William Holmes, the blacksmith and wheelwright, about 1890, and was used for funerals until 1920. Its present whereabouts is unknown.

The smithy cottages, *c.* 1950. These houses and the cottages in Ragley Drive, were some of the Digby properties in Sheldon which were sold off in 1919. The sale included shoeing shops, the engine house, the wheelwright's shop and the pigsty.

The smithy in 1967. William Holmes was a keen cricketer and is said to have played against W.G. Grace in the fields behind the church. The smithy is now a timber yard and also sells large dog kennels and rabbit hutches.

Church Road near the lychgate, looking from the Radleys, *c.* 1950. In the 1920s, the brick shed on the right was used to store a manual fire pump.

Church Road looking towards the Radleys, *c.* 1950. The houses were built in the 1930s. The bushes and trees on the left were all that remained of the leafy lane shown opposite twenty-five years earlier. They were destroyed when the road was later widened.

Church Road from the Radleys, 1925, with St Giles' church in the distance. It was then called Lyndon End because it led to the common land on the edge of the Lyndon Quarter of Bickenhill Parish.

RECTORY FARM,
SHELDON.
6 Miles from Birmingham.

FARMING STOCK.

MESSRS.

R. B. COLBOURNE & THOMPSON,
F.A.I.

Have received instructions from MR. T. EVETTS (who is leaving), To Sell by Auction

On FRIDAY, JUNE 17th, 1927.

20 BEASTS

10 Newly-calved and in-calf Cows and Heifers, Barren Cow, Five 2½ and 1½-year-old Heifers and Steers, 3 Heifer Yearlings, and 1 Shorthorn Bull.

4 Work Horses & Pony,

THE USEFUL

Agricultural Implements,

Ploughs, Harrows, Scuffles, Drill, Two 4½-in. Carts, Narrow Wheel Van, Chaffcutters, Spring Float, 2 Market Carts, 2 Narrow Wheel Lorries, "Albion" Mowing Machine, Horse Rake, Tedding Machine, 6-8 h.p. and 1½ h.p. Petrol Engines, Tackle and Harness, Dairy Utensils, POULTRY, Wood Buildings, and a portion of the

HOUSEHOLD FURNITURE

including Antique Oak Welsh Dresser, 4 Chippendale Chairs, Tables, Bedsteads, etc., etc.

---o---

SALE AT 12 O'CLOCK PROMPT.

Above: Sale details of Old Rectory farm, 1927. It was in use as the parsonage from the early 1600s to 1852 when the Revd Jones-Bateman decided it was too small for his family. It was then let to tenant farmers.

Opposite above: Old Rectory farmhouse in 1986, the focal point of Sheldon Country Park.

Opposite below: At Rectory farm, c. 1898. The elderly couple were William and Emma Cater, the tenant farmers 1880 to 1904. The young man was Thomas Evetts, their farm bailiff who eventually took over the farm tenancy. The baby was his son Tom, the last Evetts to farm here, selling up in 1927.

Church Road from the south, with Common Lane just past Jubilee Bridge, *c.* 1920. The stream is Westley Brook, which ran under the lane here from Lyndon End towards Old Rectory farm to the right.

Front view of the moat house and moat, *c.* 1920. The remains of this eighteenth century house survived to about 1960. A secret passage was said to connect the moat house and the church, but one was never found.

The moat house farm buildings, *c.* 1920. The moat was filled in around 1950 by which time it had become contaminated and foul smelling.

Jubilee Bridge and the rear of the moat house, *c.* 1920. The bridge was built to commemorate Victoria's sixty years as Queen. The stream and moat regularly flooded in winter, and in bad years Church Road was under water from the Institute to Sheaf Lane.

The Revd Jones-Bateman with Tom Evetts, *c.* 1910. He was rector from 1849 to 1910 and was regarded with respect and affection. In old age he regularly rode to church on his tricycle.

Sheldon rectory, *c.* 1925. Built in the 1820s, its main entrance was on the Coventry Road. Also known as Sheldonfield House, it was the Revd Jones-Bateman's home from 1860. It had seventeen bedrooms and a conservatory with grapevines and peach trees. The house and grounds were sold for development in 1929.

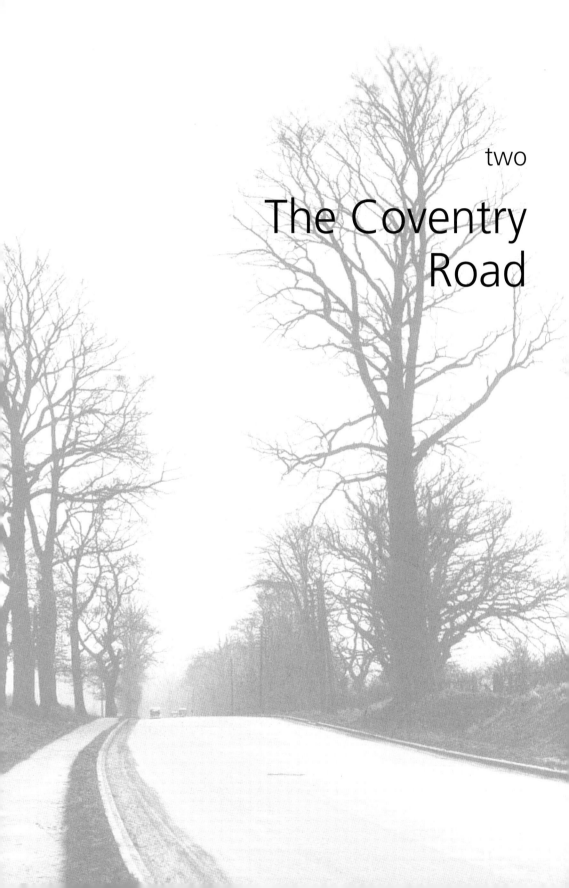

two

The Coventry Road

The Coventry Road looking south from Brays Road, 1967. On the right, the New Coventry Road was built in the early 1930s creating this island between Brays Road and Barrows Lane.

The same view in 1973, with a new pedestrian underpass to allow residents to cross this increasingly busy road. Several office blocks have since been built beyond the petrol station.

The old Coventry Road south to Barrows Lane, *c.* 1920. In 1933 this steep hill became a one-way road, with the traffic going in the opposite direction to this old car. The six terraces on the right still stand as does the central block of terraces on the left.

The cottage stores near Wagon Lane, *c.* 1925. The shop is just out of sight at the bottom of the hill on the above photograph.

The old Wagon and Horses public house, in around 1930, said to date from 1627. From the 1870s it also had Tea and Pleasure Gardens to attract a new type of customer, workers from Birmingham enjoying their Saturday half-day holiday away from the town.

Douglas Copley in his 1898 Daimler, *c.* 1930. He was landlord of the Wagon and Horses from 1923 to 1951 and collected early vehicles. He raced his cars in competitions and was a well known local character. He died in 1984 aged ninety-five.

Side view of the inn and the beginning of Wagon Lane, 1937. The hand-pump fire engine on the left came from Wootton Wawen and was part of Doug Copley's collection. The stagecoach shown on the previous page came from Moreton Morrell.

The old Coventry Road at the junction of Barrows Lane and Wagon Lane, 1937. There was a rapid growth of housing here in the 1930s.

The same view as above in 2002, with office blocks replacing some of the 1930s houses. The new public house was built in 1938 alongside the old one, which was then demolished to make the car park.

The Coventry Road towards the Wheatsheaf junction, 1967. By 1990 large office blocks had been built on both sides of the road. The open space to the left is the Lyndon End part of Sheldon Country Park, leading to Church Road.

A closer view, also 1967. This is now a very busy road, the grass verges having been lost to extra traffic lanes, with a pedestrian underpass and traffic lights.

The Sheldon cinema in 1966. From the 1920s, cinemas were very popular places of entertainment, offering glamour, adventure and escapism in every suburb, but television became a major factor in their decline. This one was demolished in 1973 and a supermarket stands here now.

The Three Horse Shoes public house surrounded by new office blocks, 1973. A bungalow style building has since replaced the old Shoes.

The Sheldona Café, near the Wheatsheaf Hotel, *c.* 1920. This area was still rural and the café was a welcome stop for walkers and cyclists on their way to Elmdon and Stonebridge. Curiously there seems to be a model lighthouse on the roof of the tea room.

The Three Horse Shoes public house, *c.* 1930. The early nineteenth-century building was retained as an extension when the large Edwardian replacement was built.

The original inn, *c.* 1885. The lady with the horse and trap may be Maria Bloxham, widow of John Bloxham, the publican from 1874. She ran the pub after him, and was succeeded by their son William who went bankrupt in 1894 and had to sell up. The Bloxhams were also farmers at Wells Green. The other woman is Sarah Berrick, who worked there.

Small Heath Harriers at the Three Horse Shoes, *c.* 1940. It was a popular base for running and cycling clubs from the early 1900s.

The Coventry Road at the Wheatsheaf junction, 1967. Shops first opened here in the 1930s to supply the new housing estates nearby. On the left a new square of shops with flats above is under construction away from the busy road.

The junction in 1976, before the installation of new traffic signals.

Looking north at the junction, *c.* 1920. The new and grand Wheatsheaf Hotel replaced a small eighteenth-century inn and provided more room for the growing local population. Like the Shoes, it also had a large bowling green at the rear.

The same view fifty years later in 1976.

Offices opposite the Parade shops, 1967. Note the bungalow stranded between two blocks. This part of the road was originally wholly residential. Commercialisation began in the 1950s in response to business generated by the airport, with taxi and car hire firms, and travel and shipping agents.

The Parade shops opposite the offices shown above, 1986.

The view north from Bantry Close, 1964. There is still a petrol station here, but large office blocks, including one occupied by the Severn Trent Water Authority, have replaced Abelson's plant works.

The view south from the same spot, 1964. The Music Box and the shop to its left have become a small hotel and restaurant. There are now many small hotels and bed and breakfast businesses in the area, entirely due to the airport and the NEC.

The Coventry Road at Hatchford Brook, 1950. The stream passes under the road just beyond the bus. The stump of the tree on the right is all that remains today of the oaks which once grew here.

The trolley bus terminal, with Arden Oak Road and Sheldonfield Road behind, 1951. The Coventry Road service to the Swan was extended here in 1936. The trolley bus route No.94 ran until 1951 when it was replaced by the No.58 motor bus.

The terminus in 1967, with Arden Oak Road in the background. Bus services now continue to the airport and the NEC.

At Hatchford Brook in 2002. The road is now a very busy dual carriageway, with speed cameras and an underpass for pedestrians. The Arden Oak pub is a recent addition to the view, built on land next to the bus shown in the photograph above.

Open ground beyond Hatchford Brook, 1967.

The same view on 31 July 1969 of the newly opened Hatchford Brook municipal golf course. The Cranes Park estate lies behind the trees on the left, close to the location of Lower Barn farm.

Near the entrance to the future golf course, on the left, 1967. There is now a wide, landscaped dual carriageway here with new office blocks on the horizon.

The view south to Elmdon from the city boundary, 1937. The airport would be built on the left.

A Good Brick and Tile Cottage and Garden,

COVENTRY ROAD,

OS. No. 168 in the Parish of Elmdon, and containing ·200 Acre, or

32 perches,

known as

"TIGER'S ISLAND COTTAGE,"

containing Living Room, Kitchen and Scullery combined, Larder, two Bedrooms, Coal-house, Pigsty with Roost over, Fowl House. There is an enclosed Yard and good water supply.

Let to Mrs. Burgess on a monthly tenancy producing a rental of

£6 10s. 0d. per annum.

There is a P.O. Wayleave for 1 stay in respect of which a rent of 6d. per annum is receivable. Tithe (apportioned value), 1d.

This Lot is sold with the benefit of a right of way over the foredrift No. pt. 169, part of Lot 37.

A well known local curiosity, Tiger's Island was a cottage on the Elmdon side of the boundary and was for sale in 1919 as part of the Digby's Coleshill estate. Eliza Burgess was the widow of the gamekeeper who lived here from 1890. The origin of the name is not known but it soon came into use as a name for the boundary itself.

View north from the boundary, 1937. On the right is the old 'green lane' to Marston Green. Just visible is a cottage in Sheldon, next to Tiger's Island in Elmdon. Both were lost to security fencing at the airport perimeter but a public footpath still leads to Marston Green, detouring around the runway.

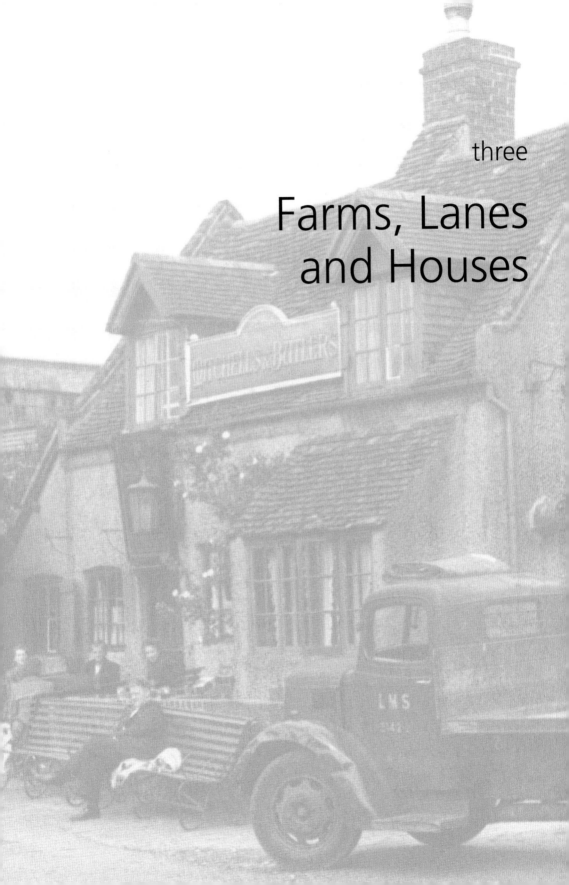

three

Farms, Lanes and Houses

The Manor House, Manor House Lane, *c.* 1920. Near the border with Yardley, this Victorian house was on the site of a medieval manor house in the Lyndon Quarter of Bickenhill. It was demolished about 1960 and replaced by maisonettes.

St Bernard's Grange, Barrows Lane, *c.* 1920. In 1919 it was described as a 'grand, old fashioned country residence' and was the home of Ambrose Wimbush, the confectioner, until his death in 1935, after which it became a public house.

Lyndon Green farm, 1933. This pretty black and white farm house dated from the seventeenth century and was located near the present Larne Road. The Eades family lived here from 1912 to 1939, when it was demolished.

An Eades' cart delivering milk in Small Heath, *c.* 1930. Fresh milk was still delivered by local farmers, ladled from churn to jug on the doorstep. In Sheldon, they would also supply eggs, chickens for the pot, and pork joints and bacon from their own pigs, killed on the farm.

Barrows Lane from the Coventry Road, 1925. Previously known as Lyndon End Lane, it roughly
marked the south-eastern boundary of the Lyndon Quarter and proceeded north to Lyndon Green.

Gilbertstone House, Lyndon, 1935. This dramatic gothic house was built in 1866 for Samuel Thornley on the hill where the modern Herondale and Saxondale Roads meet. The Thornleys were paint manufacturers in Birmingham and moved here in about 1830 into an older house, buying up land, farms and houses all over Sheldon, Elmdon and Marston Green.

Above: Sheldon Heath Road in around 1930, looking south to the Radleys from Wells farm. Low lying and with meadows on both sides, this stretch of road was originally to be called the Black Radleys.

Opposite above: Garretts Green farm, 1935. The Reeves family farmed here throughout the nineteenth century, the last being the widowed Ann Reeves, who described herself as a cow keeper. It was one of many farms in Sheldon and Tile Cross compulsorily purchased by Birmingham City Council for housing estates.

Opposite below: Wells farm at Garretts Green, *c.* 1930. The farm got its name from the Wells family who were tenant farmers here until the 1880s. Sheldon Heath Road, on the bottom left, was later extended north through this site. This country lane became the roundabout shown on page 77.

The Chestnuts, Garretts Green, 1919. The estate was acquired by Birmingham City Council in the 1930s for housing. The house was located on the hill where the church of St Thomas now stands, but the site was originally intended for the public library.

The Elms at the Radleys, c. 1890, with members of the Cattell family. They lived here from 1858 to 1928 and were related to the Cattells of Sheldon Hall. It was another Digby property sold in 1919, when it was described as a gentleman's farm residence and model homestead.

The junction of Sheldon Heath Road and the Radleys, from Church Road, *c.* 1930. There is a large traffic island here now. Brays Road was cut later, to the left of the guide post. The photograph on page 80 was taken in 1986 just ahead of this spot.

The Radleys looking towards Marston Green, *c.* 1930. Wild and bleak, it was still possible to see partridges, pheasants, wild rabbits and even stoats here.

The Bell inn, Tile Cross, *c.* 1935. Dating from 1668, it is one of Sheldon's oldest surviving inns. It was a favourite stopping place on the walk to Chelmsley Wood, when lemonade cost one penny and a pint of beer three pennies.

The Bell in 1985. A huge volume of traffic now passes this small building to and from the motorway junctions at Bickenhill and north east Birmingham. The viaduct behind supports the London to Birmingham railway line which opened in 1838 and divided Tile Cross from the rest of Sheldon.

Signpost at the junction of Bell Lane, with Tile Cross Road on the right, and Mackadown Lane on the left, *c.* 1920. The haystacks and barns belong to Malthouse farm, which was demolished in 1950. St Giles' nursing home was built roughly where the farm used to be.

Tile Cross farm, 1919. Demolished in about 1952, it stood a few yards from the White Hart down a lane which disappeared under the East Meadway. For most of the nineteenth century it was farmed by the Mayou family who also brewed and sold beer.

The White Hart inn, 1896. Said to be Sheldon's oldest pub, it still has some seventeenth-century timber framing at the front. William Jackson was the publican from about 1860 to 1896, and at one time the Jacksons had three farms in Tile Cross.

The White Hart in 1985, altered and extended. It was also known as the Tile Cross inn and the Cross and White Hart.

Sheldon Hall, 1868. This fine Jacobean house, dating from 1618, is the successor to East Hall, the medieval manor house of the Sheldon family. In 1751 it was bought by John Taylor, the Birmingham button and toy manufacturer, and co-founder of Taylor and Lloyd's bank. It was later acquired by the Digby family.

The hall in 1906, looking rather neglected. For most of the nineteenth century the hall was occupied by the Chilwell and Cattell families who farmed in the area. The monkey puzzle tree, a favourite of Victorian gardeners, had grown tall since 1868, but in 2004 it is a bare, dried up trunk.

Staircase to the first floor, *c.* 1910, showing the intricate Jacobean carving repeated throughout the house. When the Digbys sold the hall in 1919, the staircase and oak panelling were disposed of separately and disappeared.

Carved oak fireplace, 1906. This stunning fireplace stood in the old banqueting hall and was also sold off separately. In the 1980s, the hall was unoccupied and vandalised to the brink of extinction.

Above: Part of the old moat, 1935. The moat dated from the time the Sheldon family had their house here, but it had largely dried up by 1756.

Opposite above: Timber and brick interior wall, 1953. Sheldon Hall is one of the earliest local buildings to be made from brick. Now safe for the future, it is currently in use as a pub restaurant.

Opposite below: Brick fireplace, 1953. With a large timber lintel, this fireplace is set in the north wall of the hall range, the oldest part of the house.

Outmoor farm, Gressel Lane, 1935. This farmhouse dated from the early 1600s and was timber framed beneath the rough cast. It was demolished in 1950.

A steam threshing machine at Outmoor farm, *c.* 1930. Farming was hard work, with long hours and no day off. While local youngsters happily helped out at harvest time, for permanent work they preferred factories, with better pay and working conditions.

Babbs mill on the River Cole, 1936. Close to Sheldon Hall, it was probably the Lord's mill where his tenants had to send their corn to be milled. Its name comes from John Babb who was the miller in 1615.

The mill in 1983. It was still in use as a corn mill in 1889 but was converted to cottages in the 1930s. The course of the river has been altered but the mill is now next to a large lake and surrounded by public open space.

Kents Moat, 1935. By 1373 Sheldon was divided into two manors, East Hall (Sheldon Hall) and West Hall (Kents Moat). This earthwork is all that remains of West Hall, but excavations in 1964 revealed a lost manor house larger and grander than East Hall would have been. The site has been preserved within Kents Moat housing estate.

Pool Lane, c. 1935. Just north of Kents Moat, it marked the boundary with Yardley. The name has been preserved in the Poolway shopping centre.

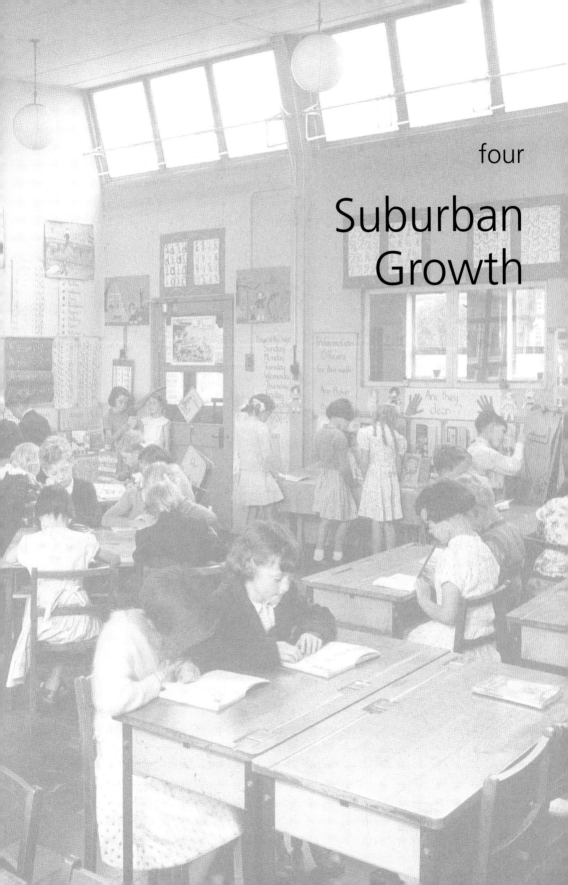

four

Suburban
Growth

Bomb damaged houses in Ivydale Avenue, 18 April 1941. The view of the church and Old Rectory farm is now hidden by trees beside Westley Brook.

German prisoners of war road building somewhere in Sheldon. The date, location and photographer are unknown. Presumably the man in the suit was the foreman responsible for the work party. It would be interesting to know more of the background to this rare photograph.

Residents of Barrows Lane and Brays Road celebrating VE Day in 1945.

The children's victory parade.

Prefabs in Common Lane, 1967. Hundreds of temporary prefabricated bungalows were built in Sheldon and Tile Cross after 1945. They were meant to last only ten years but most were still occupied in the early 1970s. They were surprisingly spacious inside, with small front and rear gardens, and most residents loved living in them.

Barrows Lane near the Grange public house, 1953.

Horrell Road coronation party, June 1953. The children's tea party was held in the garage of No. 64, owned by Richard Holloway. Note the children were all drinking free milk.

All the children were given a souvenir mug, cup, saucer and plate.

Brays Road near Horrell Road, 1967. Sheldon Community Library, on the left, was opened in 1956 when the staff were surprised to be inundated with hordes of small children eager to borrow books.

Close up of a 'steel' house, 1951. Because of the chronic shortage of materials and labour, prefabricated structures were built on some municipal estates. Many are now privately owned and their origins effectively disguised by brick cladding, pebble dashing or tiling.

Mr William Gumbley fitting the library's oak shelving.

Library interior, c. 1960. In the background is the librarian, Janet Gardner. The original formal in-and-out counters have recently been replaced by a more open, spacious and welcoming entrance area.

Comberton Road, Sheldon Heath, 1956. The provision of shops with flats above solved two shortages at once. The Co-op was often the first retailer to move into a developing area. As shopping habits changed, these units became derelict and vandalised, and have been replaced by houses and bungalows for the elderly.

Hidcote Hall tenants' club room, Garretts Green estate, 1955. The city council wanted to build community centres on all new estates but could only afford small clubrooms like this, the first of twenty-eight built in the city before 1965.

Sheldon Heath comprehensive school, 1959. After 1945, the Labour Party in Birmingham chose to experiment with mixed grammar, technical and secondary schools in areas where no secondary schools already existed. This was the first fully comprehensive school and admitted its first pupils in 1955.

Like the new schools built at Tile Cross at the same time, it was equipped with science and engineering laboratories, rooms for domestic science, music and crafts, and a separate gym block.

Garretts Green Lane at the Meadway, 1961. This was the terminus for several bus routes, and as there were no shops nearby, this little kiosk was a welcome sight for passengers, bus drivers and conductors.

Sheldon fire station under construction on the waste ground shown above.

The rear of the station with the drill tower, backing onto Outmore Road.

The junction of Garretts Green Lane and Sheldon Heath Road, 1964. On the left is the police station, opened in 1954, and on the right is the Technical College. The doctor's surgery in the centre roughly marks the site of the farm shown at the bottom of page 52.

Garretts Green Lane Technical College, 1954. Birmingham was still a major manufacturing centre after 1945 and employers wanted workers with good technical skills. Many of the students were apprentices attending day-release courses while working for organisations like the old Gas, Electricity and Water Boards.

Technical drawing class. The building today is the East Campus of the City College and caters for a much more diverse and lively body of students.

A council house interior, *c*. 1952. The sitting room and dining area are dressed in the style of a 'show home' to attract ambitious tenants with a good income. Many people transferring from the central slum districts were on low incomes and could not afford the rents of the better quality homes.

The design of the windows and door indicate that this is the interior of a brick built house in the Sheldon Heath area.

Sheldon Heath Road from the Radleys, 1986. The prefabricated Cabin public house was built in the early 1950s. The poor design of the flats on the left encouraged anti-social behaviour and they have since been replaced by much needed sheltered accommodation for the elderly.

Shops at the Radleys, c. 1955. The lack of local shops was a worry for women living in the nearby prefabs, made worse when building began on the Elms estate. A survey in 1950 revealed that Sheldon had one shop for every 228 residents, compared to the citywide average of one for every 56.

Church Road at the Radleys, seen from the tower of St Giles' church, 1967. The tall trees mark the site of the Elms, shown on page 54. This part of Church Road is also featured on page 21.

Railway viaduct across the Radleys, 1954. Prefabs were mainly built on land not wanted for permanent housing. They have now gone from here and the land has reverted to the wild space it was in the 1930s.

Mapledene primary school, newly finished in 1950. The two pre-war primary schools, at Cockshutt Hill and Stanville Road, were inadequate to cope with the post-war population explosion in Sheldon. By 1960, fifteen new schools had been built in the area.

Miss Giles' class, *c.* 1965.

The school choir, *c.* 1965.

Reading time for an infants' class, *c.* 1955.

Members of Sheldon Women's Institute, c. 1980. It was formed in 1928 when Sheldon was still a Warwickshire village, and folded in 1996. The ladies minding the stall at the church fete are, left to right, Mrs Altrincham, Harrison, Courbet, Hemmings, Horridge, Levy and Argyle.

TOTAL DEPOSIT £25 — RECTORY PARK ESTATE — TOTAL DEPOSIT £25

SHELDON

NO EXTRAS £395 NO EXTRAS

NO ROAD OR LEGAL CHARGES

THE FIRST TIME OFFERED TO THE PUBLIC

Owing to the enormous success of our Laurels Estate adjoining, we have purchased this beautiful park and propose developing it on the same lines. - - CHOOSE YOUR PLOT NOW.

Accommodation is everything that could be desired consisting of : Spacious Square Hall, Large Dining Room and Lounge, Compact Kitchen with Dresser and Washing Boiler. Outside W.C. and Coals. Three Large Bed Rooms, Landing of good dimensions, Bathroom with Tiled Walls, splendid Bath, Splash Back ; also W.C.

GARAGE SPACE.

CHOICE OF DECORATIONS AND GRATES.

SPECIAL FEATURES: Spacious Bays to all principal rooms, French Bay at rear. Roofing Tiles Torched on underside. All Chromium Taps, Copper Boiler and Circulation. Belfast Sink with Tiled Surround. Electric Fires to Bedrooms. Power Points for Cleaner and Radio. Concrete Post and Chain Front Fencing.

CONCRETE FOUNDATIONS.

WRITE OR CALL AND ASK FOR ILLUSTRATED [...]

A builder's advertisement for an estate of private houses, c. 1936. These houses were on offer for individuals to buy when it was still common for new houses to be rented out by the landowner or builder. Even the wealthy rarely owned their homes, but the 1930s saw the start of home ownership by the middle classes.

five

Around Tile Cross

Flats in Shirestone Road, newly completed in 1953. Six of these blocks were the only multi-storey flats built in Tile Cross. The land behind, which used to be a huge sand pit, has been left as open space.

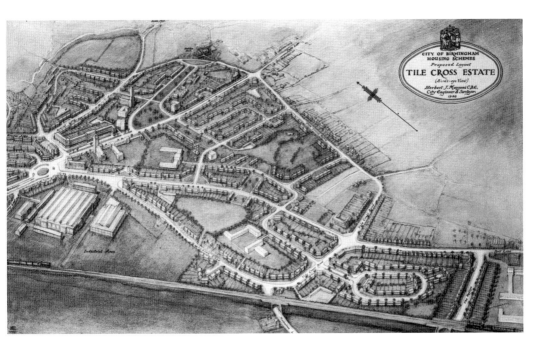

Proposed plan for the development of Tile Cross, 1946. This design, not wholly kept to,
was a break from those of previous municipal estates, noted for flattened landscapes and roads laid
out in geometric patterns.

Newly completed houses, 1952. The open appearance of Tile Cross involved building largely
traditional style houses, which it was hoped would attract upper income tenants. The average
cost of building a three bedroom council house in 1952 was £1,680. Having a proper back
garden, rather than a yard, was a bonus for many moving from inner-city terraces.

Mackadown Lane, 1963. This was a typical solution to the lack of proper social facilities in the area. There were plenty of plots of land for rent and it only needed a few enterprising residents to get a club started.

Factory in Mackadown Lane, 1961. No large-scale industry was planned for the district, but a site alongside the railway line, between Mackadown Lane and Garretts Green Lane, was allocated for small manufacturing and warehousing. A few factories opened in the 1930s.

The Central grammar school for boys, *c.* 1960. Opened in 1957, this was the first of three new secondary schools planned for Gressel Lane and allowed Central grammar to move from its old buildings in Suffolk Street, where it began life in 1897 as the Municipal Technical school.

The science laboratory.

Sir Wilfrid Martineau secondary school, officially opened in 1962. This was a mixed school for boys and girls, an arrangement which was still disputed among educationists.

The main hall, and the stage used for amateur drama by the pupils.

Byng Kendrick grammar school for girls, opened for new pupils in 1958. The secondary schools built in Birmingham in the 1950s all look very similar.

The library. Pupils who passed the 11-plus examination had the choice of attending a separate single-sex grammar school, or one of the new secondary moderns, which taught children of all abilities.

Tile Cross Road, *c.* 1930. Mackadown Lane and Tile Cross Road are the oldest roads in the Sheldon district, dating from the Anglo-Saxon period as track ways between the first fields.

Tile Cross Road, 1965. The city boundary runs across these rear gardens. Beyond is Chelmsley Wood, soon to disappear. Houses and bungalows at this spot were demolished to make Bosworth Drive, leading to the overspill development.

Shops in Tile Cross Road, 1964. The old houses on the right were next to Bennetts Well farm, now all replaced by new houses.

The view from Cooks Lane in about 1985, with Tile Cross Road on the left and East Meadway ahead. The roads here are now very busy but the White Hart, on the right, still survives. Compare this with the photograph of the White Hart on page 59.

Cooks Lane garage, 1973, now abandoned and derelict.

Prefabs in Mackadown Lane, 1967, clinging to the edge of the road in their own little avenues, to make the most use of the space.

Gossey Lane primary school, *c.* 1960, looking much as it does today. The school-building programme only just kept pace with the house-building programme, which vastly increased the number of children in the district.

School dinner was still a traditional meal of meat and vegetables, which these children were clearly enjoying and in silence too.

Above: View towards East Meadway, with Kents Moat flats and Poolway on the right, 1980. Pool Lane, shown on page 66, ran across the open ground at the rear of the flats.

Left: Poolway shopping centre, 1964, named after Pool Lane. Opened in 1957, it won praise for the new idea of incorporating a pedestrian precinct.

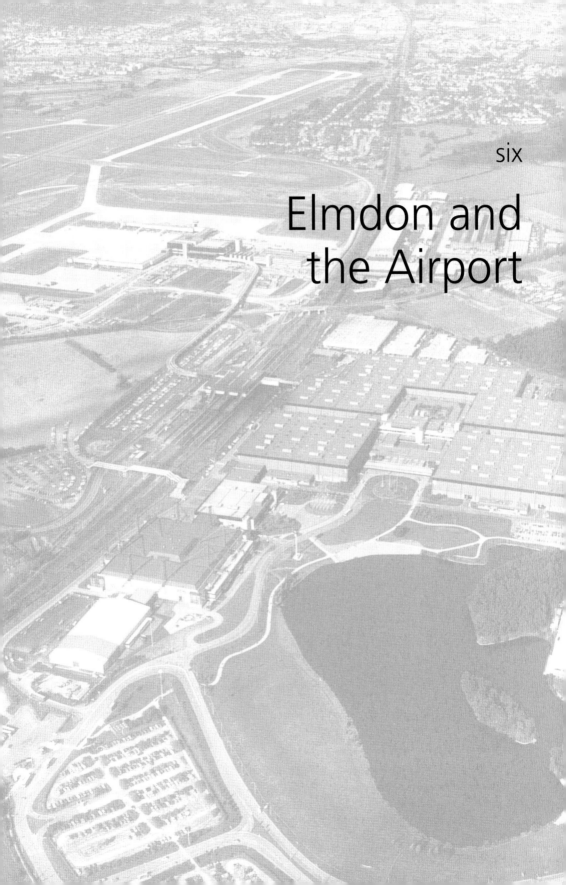

six

Elmdon and
the Airport

The Coventry Road at Elmdon, looking north to Sheldon, *c.* 1910. On the left is Damson Lane, and on the right Elmdon Lane leading to Marston Green. The little cottages on the left supplied teas to cyclists and walkers, and still stand, clinging to the edge of the A45.

Village farm, 1931. Also now on the very edge of the A45, the traffic literally runs by the front door. Both barn and house date from the 1600s.

Elmdon farm, 1919. It initially survived the construction of Elmdon airport but the lane to Marston Green was eventually closed beyond the farm house, where the hangars and runway were built.

The Coventry Road leaving the village for Sheldon, 1937. By 1947 only the two protruding wings of the ancient Cock inn remained. All the buildings on the right were eventually demolished to widen the road.

Above: Elmdon Hall, 1870. Elmdon was a small farming community when Isaac Spooner, an influential banker and manufacturer in Birmingham, moved here in the mid-eighteenth century. In 1780 he built this impressive house on the hill overlooking the village, at once raising its status. In 1834 the Alston family bought the house and manor and lived here for the next century. The last squire was a bachelor and in later life lived here alone with a dozen servants. The hall park, the church and a few cottages are all that remain of the old village today, dominated as it is by the sight and sounds of the airport and motorways.

Opposite above: The main hall in 1931. Squire Alston was succeeded by his sister but she decided to sell the estate. The hall was virtually abandoned and was demolished in 1956.

Opposite below: The rose garden in 1931. As well as extensive parkland with a large lake, now a public park, the hall had ornamental kitchen gardens, glasshouses for vines and peaches, and a tortoise house.

St Nicholas' church, 1927. With its abandoned hall and ivy-hidden church, it is not surprising that so many people walked and cycled to Elmdon to enjoy its mysterious charms. In the summer, there were fêtes and garden parties, a tradition started by Squire Alston. The church was rebuilt by Isaac Spooner and has several monuments to the family. William Wilberforce, the anti-slavery campaigner, married Barbara Spooner here in 1797.

Terrace cottages, 1933. These cottages near the rectory were generally occupied by servants of the hall, the groom, coachman, carpenter, gamekeeper and gardeners. At the nearest end is the schoolhouse, still in use in 1933.

The Chase family, *c.* 1898. Joseph Chase was the butler at the hall, and lived here with his wife Mary Ann, daughter Ethel, son Fred, and twins Clement and Hugh.

Aerial view of part of Elmdon village and the old airport, 1967. On the right is Marston Green, with the tower block flats of Chelmsley Wood and Kingshurst in the distance. On the left is the A45 at the Sheldon boundary. The old airport buildings are now a freight terminal.

The terminal under construction, March 1938. A municipal airport was first proposed in 1934 with the support of other local authorities in the area, which saw the long term benefits to the economy. Before the age of giant cranes and pre-cast concrete, the terminal was effectively built by hand.

In September 1938, the building takes shape.

The terminal almost complete, February 1939. Resembling a cross between a ship and a plane, the design was inspired by the Templehof terminal in Berlin. The airport opened for service on 1 May 1939, with twelve scheduled internal flights a day.

Midland Aero Club planes, 1939. The airfield was requisitioned by the Air Ministry on 16 September 1939 to be used by the Royal Air Force for training. Sterling and Lancaster bombers made at Marston Green were delivered here for testing before active service.

A Douglas DC-3 aircraft, *c.* 1955. This American plane, developed in 1936, became famous as the wartime Dakota, converted to carry cargo and paratroops. It was extremely reliable and could land on dirt, grass or concrete runways. The civilian version carried about twenty passengers and cruised at 185 mph. Thousands were still in use around the world in the 1960s.

An Aer Lingus DC-3, 1963. Scheduled flights between Elmdon and Dublin began in 1949, carrying passengers and freight. In exchange for fresh dairy produce, the Irish received Atco lawnmowers made in Small Heath.

Check in desk, 1962. When the airport was re-opened for civilian use in 1948, scheduled flights were restricted to destinations in western Europe. In 1962, foreign travel was still mainly for business purposes and only a few could afford to travel for pleasure.

A Vickers Viscount aircraft, c. 1960. A British made plane, it was used extensively by British European Airways from 1953. BEA carried a quarter of the air passengers travelling in Europe in the 1950s, and at a profit. The Viscount carried about sixty passengers and cruised at 323 mph.

Inside the control tower, 1960.

An essential drink before take-off, 1963, especially if passengers have seen inside the control room!

Aerial view, 1963. The terminal was extended in that year to accommodate the increase in passengers. More car park space was also needed. Behind the Excelsior Hotel, at the top of the photo, wartime huts used by the RAF are still to be seen.

A BAC-111 jet aircraft, *c.* 1965. This British short-haul jet was ideal to operate from small airports like Elmdon and was one of the few commercially successful British planes. British United Airways was established in 1960 to compete with the monopoly state airlines. This plane carried almost 100 passengers and cruised at 541 mph.

Above: Aerial view, 1983, taking in the old airport, top left, the new airport, the NEC, railway line and new station, with Pendigo Lake and the Hilton Metropole Hotel. This was the early phase of the National Exhibition Centre, with halls one to five around the Piazza, top of the lake, and the Arena, left of the lake. Pendigo Lake is artificial and was named after a farm previously here. The trading estate north of the NEC is on the site of the wartime plane factory.

Opposite above: Birmingham International Airport, 1984. The new terminal buildings are close to the old airport and the London to Birmingham railway line. Hotels, office blocks and more car parks have since been added. By the late 1980s, almost 3 million passengers passed through each year: in May 2004, there were over 600,000 passengers in just one month.

Opposite below: The Maglev transit link, 1986, connecting the NEC and mainline railway station with the airport. Maglev (from magnetic levitation) opened in 1984 to great acclaim but was hit by technical problems and was suspended in 1987. The overhead track is now used by a different and more reliable system.

The NEC Arena, 1982. The roof is supported by exterior legs, visible for some distance, to keep the interior as open as possible for conferences and concerts. The NEC is a great local success and opened in 1976. It now has twenty halls, including the Arena.

The 75th International Convention of Rotarians at the Arena, 3 June 1984. Over 22,000 Rotarians from 104 countries visited Birmingham. Trade shows at the NEC vary from building construction to footwear. Popular public shows include Crufts, Horse of the Year, Gardeners' World and the Motor Show, as well as regular events covering antiques, fashion, crafts and pop memorabilia.

seven

To the Woods

Lyndon End recreation ground, 1967. This open space is now part of Sheldon Country Park and extends from the Coventry Road to Church Road, with Westley Brook on the right.

Local schoolchildren planting bulbs in 1974, at the Church Road entrance to the park.

Ragley Drive and Old Rectory farm from the church tower, 1967. The hill to the left was the site of one of Sheldon's windmills. The Westley Brook from Lyndon Green runs by the houses on the edge of the park.

The King George the Fifth Memorial Playing Fields, 1967, now incorporated into the Country Park. The land was given in 1937 by Douglas James, a Birmingham businessman, as part of a national memorial to the late king.

Above: One of the pigsties at Old Rectory farm. Volunteers of all ages and abilities help with the everyday care of the animals, supervised by the head ranger and his staff.

Opposite above: Old Rectory farm from the park. The Country Park opened in 1986 and covers 240 acres of land extending from the Coventry Road to the railway line at Marston Green.

Opposite below: The Jersey cows indoors on a very sunny day in 2004. The farm also has horses, goats, pigs, geese and chickens.

The footbridge over Westley Brook in 1967, connecting Mapledene Road and Elmstead Road.

Marston Green railway station, 1926. The car was about to cross the track into Elmdon Lane, hopefully missing the chicken ahead! The station was little used before the 1950s as most of the locals were farm workers.

The old Post Office in Station Road, August 1909. The poster proclaims floods in Mexico and plans to outlaw the abuses of home working.

Alcott Hall, near Chelmsley Wood, 1901. In 1963, Birmingham was given permission to build over 20,000 overspill dwellings in this area, to ease its housing crisis. The house has survived, now surrounded by roads, houses, schools and shops.

Marston Green Cottage Homes, 1896. They opened in 1880 to house orphaned and abandoned children from Birmingham's workhouse. Birmingham's presence in rural north Warwickshire could be beneficial: from 1913 Marston Green was supplied with gas and water by the city.

The original sixteen cottages housed almost 500 children, living in groups with foster parents, to give a feel of family life. The children were taught a trade so they could earn a living when they left at the age of fourteen.

The regime was strict but there was time for play and exercise. The country air was healthier than the smoke of the city. As well as the school, there was also a hospital, chapel, swimming pool, farm and workshops.

A football team in 1928. By 1930, fewer children were cared for in homes, the authorities preferring to board children with families. The homes closed in 1933, but were quickly adapted for use as a mental hospital.

In 1940, the No.1 Canadian General Hospital was built next to the old cottage homes. Intended to treat military casualties, its first patients were sick babies evacuated from Birmingham hospitals and children from the Coventry Blitz. The chaplain was Father Bill Casson of the Royal Canadian Army Medical Corps.

The hospital consisted of sixteen ward huts around an oval parade ground. They will be familiar to many Birmingham residents, as in 1948 they became the maternity hospital. The cyclist is Earl Hann, who photographed his fellow Canadians during their time here.

In 1941, the Medical Corps' pipe band took part in Marston Green's War Weapons Week parade. Most of these men were originally from Scotland, and worked for Sun Life Assurance in Montreal.

A visit by the local Air Raid Precautions unit, October 1941. The Medical Corps followed the Allies onto mainland Europe and had distinguished service during the invasion of Italy in 1943.

A spring scene in Chelmsley Wood, 1892. This is probably the main footpath from Alcott Hall to Keeper's Lodge, now lost under Dunster Road. One of the last remnants of the Forest of Arden, Chelmsley Wood was described in 1822 as the 'beautiful hanging wood' of Coleshill. A small part remains in Meriden Park in the new town of Chelmsley Wood.

The wood in summer, 1910. Most of the trees were oak, birch, mountain ash and poplar, with a thick ground cover of bracken and ferns.

Picking bluebells, *c.* 1925. Every summer until the 1960s, children and adults walked and cycled from all around the Sheldon district to explore this magical place.

Other Birmingham titles published by Tempus

If you are interested in purchasing other books published by Tempus, or in case you have difficulty finding any Tempus books in your local bookshop, you can also place orders directly through our website   www.tempus-publishing.com